SINGER'S BOOK OF JAZZ STANDARDS

MEN'S EDITION

50 Great Songs in Custom Vocal Arrangements and Singer-Friendly Keys
with Traditional and Alternate Chord Changes

Arranged by Steve Rawlins

T0052550

ISBN 0-634-04967-4

HAL•LEONARD®
CORPORATION

7777 W. BLUEMOUND RD. P.O. BOX 13819 MILWAUKEE, WI 53213

Visit Hal Leonard Online at
www.halleonard.com

Steve Rawlins, arranger/pianist/clinician, has created music for the Academy Awards® and Emmy Awards™, the Olympics and the Super Bowl, and for national advertisers such as Kellogg's, Libby's and Sears. His television work has been heard on "The Tonight Show With Jay Leno", "News Radio" and "Just Shoot Me." He has arranged and performed extensively for a variety of musicians, working with such jazz artists as Benny Goodman, Steve March Tormé, George Bugatti and Laurindo Almeida.

Preface

All fifty arrangements of jazz standards in this book are written in a single line "fake book" or "lead sheet" format. However, they are not just the standard renditions of the songs. All are custom arrangements, designed especially for singers, with introductions, logical suggestions for repeated sections, and simple but stylish song endings.

The chords below the lines are the traditional harmonies. The chords above the line are more advanced, alternate harmonies. A musician using these arrangements may use just one set of these chord changes, or a mixture of them within a song.

A majority of men singers will find the chosen keys to be quite comfortable, rarely going especially high or low. They often fall into what could be called a "bari-tenor" range. There are certainly voices naturally lower than this range, and those with a higher range. Those singers will perhaps need to consider further transpositions in some cases. Many accompanying musicians can transpose a step up or down while reading the chords.

There are occasional style and performance suggestions in the arrangements, and rehearsal letters to indicate the beginning of an important phrase. There are plenty of jazz standards that do not have a verse, but for those that do, we included it.

These fifty classic songs are a perfect basis for any singer's work, whether it is as a devoted amateur or a seasoned pro. They are truly songs for a lifetime.

CONTENTS

All or Nothing at All

Men's Key

Words by Jack Lawrence
Music by Arthur Altman

Easy Swing Or Bossa

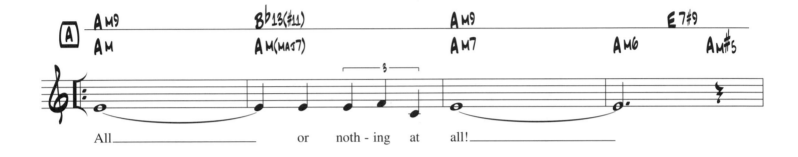

All___ or noth-ing at all!___

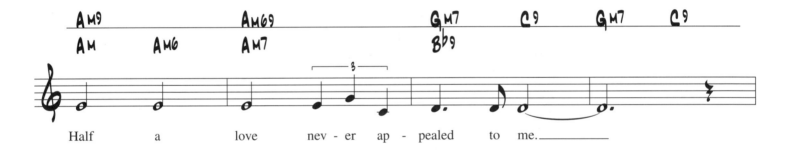

Half a love nev-er ap-pealed to me.___

If your heart nev-er could yield to me,___ then I'd

rath-er have noth-ing at all!

Alright, Okay, You Win

Men's Key

Words and Music by Sid Wyche and Mayme Watts

Autumn In New York

Men's Key

Words and Music by Vernon Duke

Moderately

Fmaj7/C Gm7(b5)/C Fmaj9/C Dm7 Gm7 A°/G C7

A
Gm9 Am7 Bbmaj9 C13 C9(#5) Fmaj9 D7sus4 D9
Gm7 Am7 Gm7 C13 Fmaj7 Am7 D9

Au-tumn in New York,_____ why does it seem-so in-vit ing?_____
Au-tumn in New York,_____ the gleam-ing roof-tops at sun-down.

Gm9 Am7 Bbmaj9 C13 C9(#5)/Bb Am11(b5) Eb9(#11) D7b9
Gm7 Am7 Gm7 C13 Am7(b5) D7sus4 D9

Au-tumn in New York,_____ it spells the thrill of first night-ing._____
Au-tumn in New York,_____ it lifts you up when you're run-down._____

B
C11 C9 F11 Eb11 Eb13 Abmaj9 D7b9#5 G7b9
Gm7 Bbm7 Eb6 Abmaj7 G9

Glit-ter-ing crowds and shim-mer-ing clouds in can-yons of steel,_____ they're
Jad-ed rou-és and gay di-vor-cees who lunch at the Ritz,_____ will

Cm9 Cm/Bb Am9 D13(b9) G11 G13 C7sus4 C9 F#m9
Cm7 Dm7(b5) G13 Cmaj7 Am7 Abm7

mak-ing me feel_____ I'm home. It's
tell you that "It's_____ di-vine!" This

Body And Soul

Men's Key

Words by Edward Heyman, Robert Sour and Frank Eyton
Music by John Green

But Beautiful

Men's Key

Words by Johnny Burke
Music by Jimmy Van Heusen

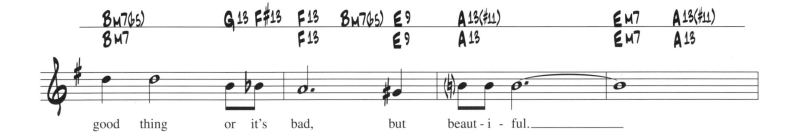

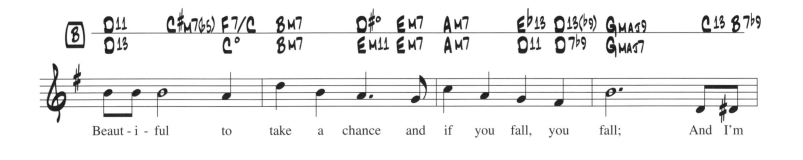

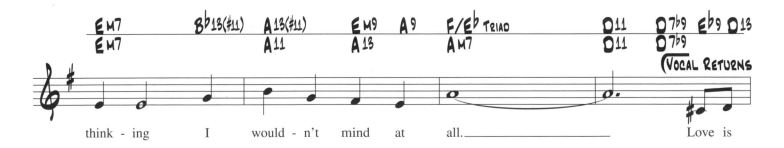

Cheek to Cheek

Words and Music by Irving Berlin

Words and Music by Irving Berlin

Men's Key

Ev'ry Time We Say Goodbye

Men's Key

FROM SEVEN LIVELY ARTS

Words and Music by Cole Porter

We love each oth-er so deep-ly, that I ask you this, sweet-heart, why should we quar-rel ev-er, why can't we be e-nough clev-er, nev-er to part.

Ev-'ry time we say good-bye, I die a lit-tle,

Day By Day

Theme from the Paramount Television Series Day By Day

Men's Key

Words and Music by Sammy Cahn, Axel Stordahl and Paul Weston

Easy Swing

(2X Solo)

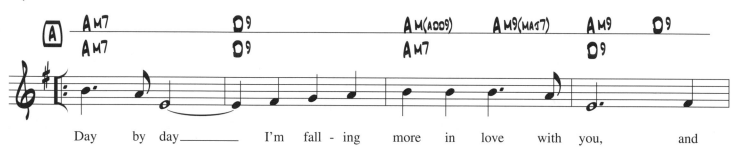

Day by day_____ I'm fall-ing more in love with you, and

day by day_____ my love seems to grow._____ There

is-n't an-y end to my de-vo-tion;_____ it's

deep-er, dear, by far than an-y o-cean._____ I find that

Do Nothin' Till You Hear From Me

Men's Key

Words and Music by Duke Ellington
and Bob Russell

Moderately Slow Swing

Do noth-in' till you hear from me. Pay no at-ten-tion to what's said, why peo-ple tear the seam of an-y-one's dream___ ___ is o-ver my head.___ Do noth-in' till you hear from me. At least con-sid-er our ro-mance; if you should take the word of oth-ers you've heard,___ I have-n't a chance.___ True I've been

seen with some-one new___ but does that mean that I'm un-true;___ when we're a-

part___ the words in my heart___ re-veal how I feel___ a-bout you.___ Some kiss may cloud my mem-o-

ry, and oth-er arms may hold a thrill, But please do noth-in' till you

hear it from me,_____ and you nev-er will.___ (Do noth-in' till you hear from)

hear it from me,_____ and you nev-er will.___ But please do noth-in' till you

(Break)

hear it from me,_____ and you nev-er will.___

Do You Know What It Means To Miss New Orleans

Men's Key

Lyric by Eddie De Lange
Music by Louis Alter

Men's Key · Don't Get Around Much Anymore

Words and Music by Duke Ellington
and Bob Russell

Missed the Sat-ur-day dance, heard they crowd-ed the floor, could-n't bear it with-out__ __ you,__ don't get a-round much an-y more. Thought I'd vis-it the club, got as far as the door, they'd have ask'd me a-bout__ __ you,__ don't get a-round much an-y more. (Well)

Fly Me to the Moon
(In Other Words)
Featured in the Motion Picture ONCE AROUND

Men's Key

Words and Music by Bart Howard

Hello, Young Lovers

FROM THE KING AND I

Men's Key

Lyrics by Oscar Hammerstein II
Music by Richard Rodgers

Jazz Waltz

36

The Frim Fram Sauce

Men's Key

Words and Music by Joe Ricardel
and Redd Evans

Gee Baby, Ain't I Good To You

Men's Key

Words by Don Redman and Andy Razaf
Music by Don Redman

Slow and Bluesy

Love___ makes me treat you the way___ that I do, gee ba-by, ain't I good___ to

you! There's noth - in' too good for a girl___ that's so true,

gee ba-by, ain't I good___ to you!

Bought you a fur coat for Christ - mas, a dia-mond ring,___
I served you___ can-dle-light din-ers and break-fast in bed,

Have You Met Miss Jones?

Men's Key

From I'd Rather Be Right

Words by Lorenz Hart
Music by Richard Rodgers

Honeysuckle Rose

Men's Key

FROM AIN'T MISBEHAVIN'
FROM TIN PAN ALLEY

Words by Andy Razaf
Music by Thomas "Fats" Waller

I Get Along Without You Very Well
(Except Sometimes)

Men's Key

Words and Music by Hoagy Carmichael
Inspired by a poem written by J.B. Thompson

Slowly or Easy Bossa

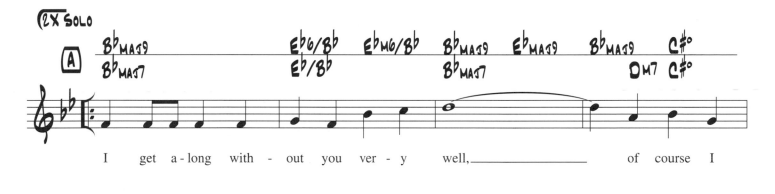

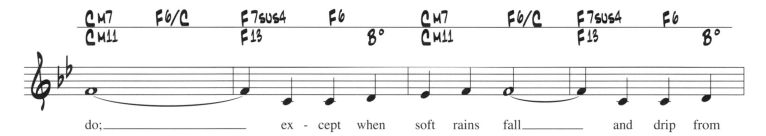

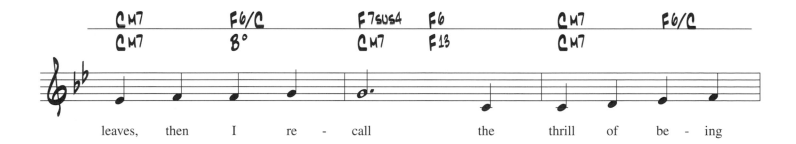

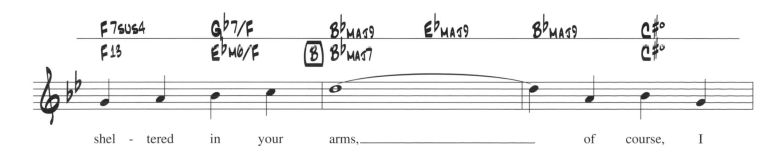

I Could Write A Book

FROM PAL JOEY

Men's Key

Words by Lorenz Hart
Music by Richard Rodgers

Easy Swing

If they

A (2X SOLO)

asked me I could write a book_____ a-bout the

way you walk and whis-per and look._____ I could

B

write a pre-face on how we met, so the

world would nev-er for-get._____ (VOCAL RETURNS) And the

I Got It Bad and That Ain't Good

Men's Key

Words by Paul Francis Webster
Music by Duke Ellington

I'm Beginning To See The Light

Men's Key

Words And Music By Don George, Johnny Hodges, Duke Ellington And Harry James

I've Got My Love To Keep Me Warm

Men's Key

FROM THE 20TH CENTURY FOX MOTION PICTURE ON THE AVENUE

Words and Music by Irving Berlin

I've Got the World on a String

Men's Key

Lyric by Ted Koehler
Music by Harold Arlen

Easy Swing

It Might As Well Be Spring

Men's Key

FROM STATE FAIR

Lyrics by Oscar Hammerstein II
Music by Richard Rodgers

Moderately – Opt. Samba

I'm as rest-less as a wil-low in a wind-storm, I'm as jump-y as a pup-pet on a string. I'd say that I had spring-fe-ver, but I know it is-n't Spring. I am star-ry eyed and vague-ly dis-con-tent-ed, like a night-in-gale with-out a song to sing. Oh, why should I have spring-fe-ver when it is-n't e-ven Spring? I keep wish-ing I were some-where else, walk-ing down a strange new street,

61

I've Got You Under My Skin

Men's Key

from Born to Dance

Words and Music by Cole Porter

Easy Swing or Bossa

got you_____ un-der my skin,_____ I've

got you_____ deep in the heart of me,_____ so

deep in my heart,_____ you're real-ly a part of me,_____ I've

got you_____ un-der my skin._____ I've

Arranged by Rawlins with homage to Nelson Riddle

B♭M7	B♭M/A♭	GM7(♭5)	C7#9#5	FM7		B♭9
B♭M7	E♭9	A♭7♭9	D♭MAJ7	D♭6	FM7	E°

know, lit - tle fool,_____ you nev-er can win,_____ use your men -

E♭M11	D°	E♭M11	A♭7(#5)	D♭MAJ9		D♭11	D♭13(♭9)
E♭M11	A♭13	E♭M11	D9(♭5)	D♭MAJ7	D♭6	A♭M7	D♭7♭9

tal - i - ty,_____ wake up to re - al - i - ty."_____ But each

GM7(♭5)		C7#9#5		FM11	B9	B♭7sus4 B♭7♭9
G♭6		G♭M6		D♭6/A♭	D♭6	B13 B♭9

time I do, just the thought of you makes me stop, be-fore I be - gin, 'cause I've

E♭13	E♭9(#5)	A♭11	A♭13(♭9)	1. D♭6
E♭M9		G♭M/A♭		

got you_____ un-der my skin._____ (I've)_____

2. D♭6	D♭6/C	B♭M7	D♭6/A♭	E♭M9	G♭M/A♭	D♭6

skin._____ Yeah, you grab me,___ un - der my skin!

(UNISON

Just One More Chance

Men's Key

Words by Sam Coslow
Music by Arthur Johnston

66

The Late, Late Show

Men's Key

Words and Music by Murray Berlin
and Roy Alfred

Lean Baby

Men's Key

Lyric by Roy Alfred
Music by Billy May

Lost Mind

Men's Key

Words and Music by Percy Mayfield

you could be so kind to help me find my mind, I'd like to thank you in ad-vance. Know

this be-fore you start my soul's been torn a-part, I lost my mind in a wild ro-mance. My

fu-ture is my past its mem-o-ry will last, I'll live to love the days gone by. Each

day that comes and goes is like the one be-fore, my mind is lost 'til the day I die. Words would

Lush Life

Men's Key

Words and Music by Billy Strayhorn

Manhattan

FROM THE BROADWAY MUSICAL THE GARRICK GAIETIES

Men's Key

Words by Lorenz Hart
Music by Richard Rodgers

Freely

Sum-mer jour-neys to Ni-ag-'ra and to oth-er plac-es ag-gra-

vate all our cares; we'll save our fares;

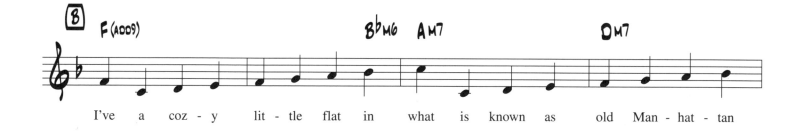

I've a coz-y lit-tle flat in what is known as old Man-hat-tan

we'll set-tle down right here in town:

My Funny Valentine

Men's Key

Words by Lorenz Hart
Music by Richard Rodgers

* This verse is normally only sung by women, provided here for information.

My One And Only Love

Men's Key

Words by Robert Mellin
Music by Guy Wood

My Romance

FROM JUMBO

Men's Key

Words by Lorenz Hart
Music by Richard Rodgers

Moderate

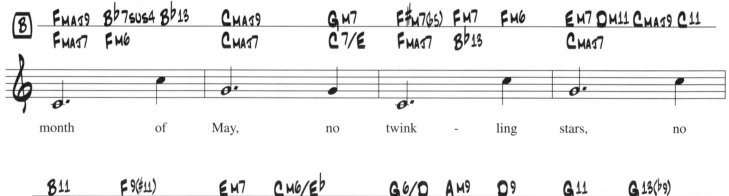

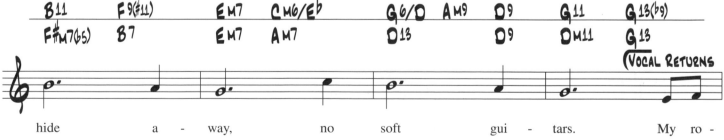

Nature Boy

Men's Key

Words and Music by Eden Ahbez

89

The Nearness Of You

FROM THE PARAMOUNT PICTURE ROMANCE IN THE DARK

Men's Key

Words by Ned Washington
Music by Hoagy Carmichael

A Nightingale Sang In Berkeley Square

Men's Key

Lyric by Eric Maschwitz
Music by Manning Sherwin

'Round Midnight

Men's Key

Words by Bernie Hanighen
Music by Thelonious Monk and Cootie Williams

Moderately slow, In 2

Route 66

Men's Key

By Bobby Troup

September Song

FROM THE MUSICAL PLAY KNICKERBOCKER HOLIDAY

Men's Key

Words by Maxwell Anderson
Music by Kurt Weill

Skylark

Men's Key

Words by Johnny Mercer
Music by Hoagy Carmichael

Moderately

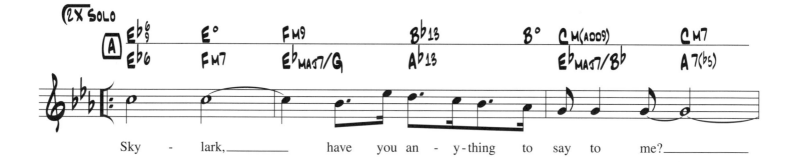

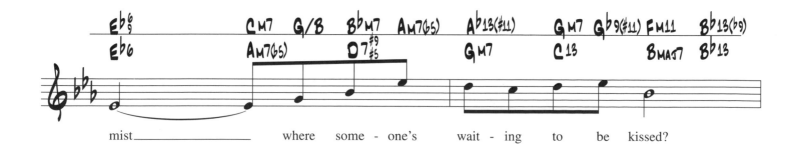

105

Speak Low

FROM THE MUSICAL PRODUCTION ONE TOUCH OF VENUS

Men's Key

Words by Ogden Nash
Music by Kurt Weill

Solitude

Words by Eddie De Lange and Irving Mills
Music by Duke Ellington

sit in my chair, I'm filled with des-pair, there's no one could be so sad._____ With

gloom ev-'ry-where I sit and I stare, I know that I'll soon go mad. In my

sol-i-tude_____ I'm pray_____ing, Dear

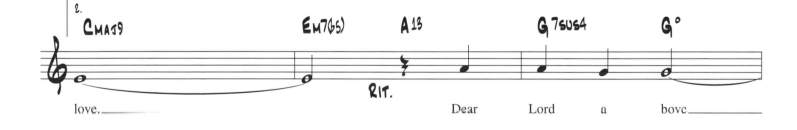

Lord a-bove_____ send back my love._____ (In my)

love._____ Dear Lord a-bove_____

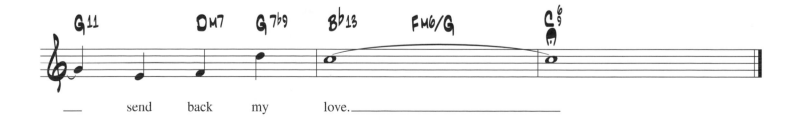

_____ send back my love._____

Stardust

Men's Key

Words by Mitchell Parish
Music by Hoagy Carmichael

...And now the pur-ple dusk of twi-light time steals a-cross the mead-ows of my heart. High up in the sky the lit-tle stars climb, Al - ways re-mind-ing me that we're a-part.

You wan-dered down the lane and far a-way, leav-ing me a song that will not die. Love is now the star-dust of yes-ter-day, the mus-ic of the years gone by._____ Some-times I

113

Where Or When

From Babes In Arms

Men's Key

Words By Lorenz Hart
Music By Richard Rodgers

Rubato

When you're a-wake the things you think come from the dreams you dream.

Thought has wings, and lots of things are sel-dom what they seem.

Some - times you think you've lived be - fore all that you live to - day.

Things you do come back to you, as though they knew the

way. Oh, the tricks your mind can play!

This Can't Be Love

FROM THE BOYS FROM SYRACUSE

Men's Key

Words by Lorenz Hart
Music by Richard Rodgers

Easy Swing

Lyrics:
This can't be love be-cause I feel so well,___ no sobs, no sor-rows, no sighs.___

This can't be love I get no diz-zy spell.___ My head is not___ in the skies.___ My heart does

What's New

Men's Key

Words by Johnny Burke
Music by Bob Haggart

When Sunny Gets Blue

Men's Key

Lyric by Jack Segal
Music by Marvin Fisher

Slow Blues Tempo

When

(2X SOLO

A

Sun-ny gets blue, her eyes get gray and cloud-y, then the rain be-gins to fall.____

Pit-ter pat-ter, pit-ter-pat-ter, love is gone so what can mat-ter? No sweet lov-er man comes to call.____ When

B

Sun-ny gets blue, she breathes a sigh of sad-ness, like the wind that stirs the trees.____

Wind that sets the leaves to sway-in'; Like some vi-o-lins are play-in' weird and haunt-ing mel-o - dies.

Witchcraft

Men's Key

Lyric by Carolyn Leigh
Music by Cy Coleman

Arranged by Rawlins with homage to Nelson Riddle

You Took Advantage of Me

Men's Key

FROM PRESENT ARMS

Words by Lorenz Hart
Music by Richard Rodgers